THE UNEASY CONSCIENCE
of
MODERN FUNDAMENTALISM

THE UNEASY CONSCIENCE

of

MODERN FUNDAMENTALISM

Carl F. H. Henry

William B. Eerdmans Publishing Company
Grand Rapids, Michigan / Cambridge, U.K.

© 1947 Wm. B. Eerdmans Publishing Company

Wm. B. Eerdmans Publishing Co.
255 Jefferson Ave. S.E., Grand Rapids, Michigan 49503 /
P.O. Box 163, Cambridge CB3 9PU U.K.

First edition 1947
This edition 2003

Printed in the United States of America

08 07 06 05 04 03   7 6 5 4 3 2 1

Library of Congress Cataloging-in-Publication Data

Henry, Carl Ferdinand Howard, 1913-
The uneasy conscience of modern fundamentalism / Carl F. H. Henry.
p.   cm.
Originally published: 1947.
Includes bibliographical references.
ISBN 0-8028-2661-X (pbk.)
1. Modernist-fundamentalist controversy.
2. Church and social problems.   I. Title.

BT82.3.H445   2003
270.8′2 — dc21

2003054329

www.eerdmans.com

To T. Leonard Lewis

Christian Friend and Former Colleague

Contents

CONTENTS

Foreword

There are some books that are important to keep in print simply because they serve as instructive museum pieces. They give us glimpses into bygone eras, helping us to grasp the insights of creative thinkers who once wrestled with questions that are very different than the ones we presently face.

The Uneasy Conscience of Modern Fundamentalism is no mere museum piece. To be sure, it has some museum-like qualities. It is clearly a book written for the late 1940s. A devastating world war had recently ended, and many Americans were thinking about new cultural challenges, both national and international. Carl F. H. Henry and others who would soon come to be known as the leaders of a "neo-evangelicalism" were deeply concerned that those Christians known as "fundamentalists" or "evangelicals" — the terms were interchangeable at the time — were ill-equipped to address the crucial issues of the day. This book is both a detailed complaint about evangelical failures and a call to renewal. And while both the complaints and the urgings for change are obviously meant for cultural conditions that were quite different from our own, there is much in this little book that can continue to instruct and inspire all of us who care deeply about the cause of the Gospel.

Needless to say, my fondness for this book has something to do with institutional pride. It was published in 1947, the year Fuller Theological Seminary began, and Carl Henry was one of our founding faculty members. The book was introduced with some brief comments by Harold John Ockenga, Fuller's founding president, and it is clear that both Henry and Ockenga saw the book as setting an agenda of sorts for their fledgling theological school. I refer to this book often when I am called upon to explain the spirit that gave birth to Fuller Seminary. All of the major elements of that founding vision are here in these pages: a deep commitment to a new kind of evangelical scholarship that would wrestle seriously with the important issues being raised in the large world of the mind; a hope for a more open evangelicalism that would transcend the barriers that had been erected by a separatistic mentality; and a profound desire to engage culture in all of its created complexity.

My own affection for this book, however, long predates

my association with Fuller Seminary. I first read it as a college student in the late 1950s, and it is one of the books that has had a profound impact on my thinking. When I went on to graduate school, I was forced to deal with an intellectual agenda that was far more complex than anything I had ever faced before. And I was presented with these new challenges just as the turmoil of "the radical 60s" began to pervade campus life. I felt ill-prepared for all of this by my spiritual upbringing, and I was seriously tempted to abandon my evangelical convictions as irrelevant to the new world I was experiencing. But the memory of the case that Carl Henry had made in this little book was a steadying influence for me. Yes, the evangelicalism of the past half-century or so had failed in its intellectual and cultural obligations. But there was hope! Not only was it *possible* to promote an intellectually and culturally engaged evangelicalism, but a worldview based solidly on biblical authority was desperately *needed* in a social climate where the current theological options had in their own ways failed to provide satisfying answers to the deepest questions of the human spirit.

In that time when I greatly needed a bit of evangelical encouragement, I was encouraged in very specific ways by the contents of this book. In probing the dimensions of evangelicalism's "uneasy conscience," both Ockenga and Henry had already in the 1940s pointed to items that would later become key matters of social and political concern. In listing actual examples of evangelical failure, each of them had accused their fellow evangelicals of being on the wrong side of such issues as war, race, class, and "imperialism." Their willingness to name these particular concerns, more than a decade before they had come to loom large in my life, was important to me when I found myself in the cultural trenches during the 1960s.

None of that gets us much beyond museum-piece status, however. In what ways does this book still speak to us today? On a superficial level, it might seem that Henry's call for an evangelical activism that recognizes the need for a broad cultural involvement is no longer necessary. In the 1970s, some thirty years after the publication of this book, a major newsmagazine featured a cover story that proclaimed in bold letters that America was experiencing "the year of the evangelical." And today the notion of a socially active evangelicalism is taken for granted. Indeed, the irony is that liberal Protestants, who once chided evangelicals for their lack of involvement in public life, are probably praying these days that the evangelical movement would revert to its otherworldly patterns!

But, the truth be told, Bible-believing Christianity still suffers to some degree from an uneasy conscience. Carl Henry's call to action in the 1940s was not a mere summons to activism. It was an invitation to an evangelical cultural involvement that was based solidly on the kind of profound theological reflection that could only be sustained by a social program that was closely linked to a systematic commitment to the nurturing of the life of the mind. And while the evangelical academy has known much scholarly success in recent decades, there is often a considerable disconnect between grassroots evangelical activism and carefully reasoned theological orthodoxy. The agenda that Henry laid out in this book still deserves sustained attention.

It must also be said that his actual suggestions as to what is required in a well-formed biblical orthodoxy continue to ring true for many of us. While there is much to celebrate in the successes of evangelicalism in recent years — both in grassroots ministries and in scholarly contributions — there are also reasons to worry a bit about tendencies in all sectors of contemporary evangelical life to dilute the proclamation of the Gospel, as well as to negotiate too-easy settlements between evangelical thought and various manifestations of our "postmodern" culture. Carl Henry's antidote to the deviations from biblical truth in the 1940s speaks also to our own day. Christian cultural involvement in the multiple spheres of human interaction must continue to be articulated within what he labeled a "supernaturalistic framework." Our basic condition as human beings has not changed since the 1940s. We are — as Carl Henry states with uncompromising clarity in these pages — rebels against the living God who are desperately in need of the regeneration that has been graciously made available to us through the finished work at Calvary. Only by diligently working out the implication of that profound perspective on the nature of things can we hope to see our own uneasy consciences transformed into hearts that long to serve the One who rules with sovereign power over all creation.

2003   RICHARD J. MOUW

a level that gives significance again to human life. It was the rediscovery of classic ancient philosophy that gave incentive to Renaissance humanism with its disastrous implications for Western culture. The hour is ripe now, if we seize it rightly, for a rediscovery of the Scriptures and of the meaning of the Incarnation for the human race.

Further, Fundamentalism is a constant object of surgery anyway. One can hardly move about the campuses of the large universities and secular colleges — let alone some religious schools — without awareness of the constant assault on our position. Numbers of clergymen who minister to university students repudiate the doctrine of substitutionary atonement as doing violence to man's moral sense. [To us who insist on the abnormality of man's religious affections, there is no infallibility of man's moral sense. The latter leads away from redemption's path those who walk in the confidence of man's inherent goodness. One of the things which modern man most needs to be saved from, is a moral sense which is outraged at a divine provision of redemption.] But it is not this doctrinal assault on the central affirmations of our faith that here distresses me; it must always be, preceding that future day when we shall no longer move by faith, that revelational and non-revelational views shall stand in sharp conflict. What concerns me more is that we have needlessly invited criticism and even ridicule, by a tendency in some quarters to parade secondary and sometimes even obscure aspects of our position as necessary frontal phases of our view. To this extent we have failed to oppose the full genius of the Hebrew-Christian outlook to its modern competitors. With the collapse of Renaissance ideals, it is needful that we come to a clear distinction, as evangelicals, between those basic doctrines on which we unite in a supernaturalistic world and life view and the area of differences on which we are not in agreement while yet standing true to the essence of Biblical Christianity. But even beyond this, I voice my concern because we have not applied the genius of our position constructively to those problems which press most for solution in a social way. Unless we do this, I am unsure that we shall get another world hearing for the Gospel. That we can continue for a generation or two, even as a vital missionary force, here and there snatching brands from the burning, I do not question. But if we would press redemptive Christianity as the obvious solution of world problems, we had better busy ourselves with explicating the solution. I am not unmindful of constructive efforts along this line, as Dr. Earle V. Pierce's *The Church and World Conditions,* but I cannot set aside the conviction that we have not as a movement faced up with the seriousness of our predicament.

Moreover, I am well aware that some who have no sympathy for a supernaturalistic viewpoint, will likely distort and misrepresent the sentiments voiced in these pages. But I do not consider it needful on that account to hesitate. Those who read with competence will know that the "uneasy conscience" of which I write is not one troubled about the great Biblical verities, which I consider the only outlook capable of resolving our problems, but rather one distressed by the frequent failure to apply them effectively to crucial problems confronting the modem mind. It is an application of, not a revolt against, fundamentals of the faith, for which I plead.

That it may be somewhat optimistic to speak of a widespread uneasiness, I also recognize. Many of our Bible institutes, evangelical colleges, and even seminaries, seem blissfully unaware of the new demands upon us. My hope is that some, who were not troubled at the outset of these pages, will become concerned before they finish.

One last word is almost superfluous. It will be almost too evident that the formulation of a solution requires much more constructive treatment. At times, I have been content with a minimal statement, seeking to provoke a united effort, rather than to dogmatize. I address my words to fellow evangelicals, in the hope that they shall not make every faltering word an occasion of calumny, but rather inviting them to stand firm in the recognition that, while we are pilgrims here, we are ambassadors also.

These chapters were delivered, in a somewhat briefer form, as a series of popular lectures in Gordon College of Theology and Missions.

1947   CARL F. H. HENRY

Introduction

Recently, when preaching a sermon on "The Influence of the Church in the Labor Crisis," I evoked a comment from a Christian soldier. Said he, "I became a political liberal on my knees, though I am a Fundamentalist in faith. Why must the church be on the wrong side of every major social issue?" Another soldier wrote, "That is a new note in Fundamentalism."

If the Bible-believing Christian is on the wrong side of social problems such as war, race, class, labor, liquor, imperialism, etc., it is time to get over the fence to the right side. The church needs a progressive Fundamentalism with a social message.

If Acts 15:13-18 outlines God's program and premillenarianism is correct, the church will not preach on Paris Conferences or liquor, yet it will not be indifferent to these pulse-beats of the world's life. If we vacillate between Fundamentalist isolationism and cooperation with the World Council of Churches, it is because we cannot be fatalistic on ethical problems. Yet Fundamentalism is precisely that. Dr. Henry has put his finger on what is troubling us. May this brief thesis be the harbinger of a new articulation of the growing revolt in evangelical circles on ethical indifferentism. It is impossible to shut the Jesus of pity, healing, service, and human interest from a Biblical theology. The higher morality of redemption does not invalidate moral consistency.

That there is little agreement concerning the Kingdom is shown from the contrast between writings of Stanley Jones and A. C. Gaebelein. It has always been easiest for me to think of the Kingdom as one, but with several forms — theocratic, church, millennial — but *all* the Kingdom of God. Unless the continuity and the breaks, along with coterminous principles and ends, of the forms of the Kingdom are recognized this question becomes a hopeless puzzle to men.

A Christian world- and life-view embracing world questions, societal needs, personal education ought to arise out of Matt. 28:18-21 as much as evangelism does. Culture depends on such a view, and Fundamentalism is prodigally dissipating the Christian culture accretion of centuries, a serious sin. A sorry answer lies in the abandonment of social fields to the secularist.

CHAPTER I

The Evaporation of Fundamentalist Humanitarianism[1]

The present tendency of conservative Christianity is to make much of the embarrassment of religious modernism.

The modernist embarrassment is serious indeed. The shallow insistence on inevitable world progress and on man's essential goodness has been violently declared false. Not only sound Bible exegesis but the world events of 1914-1946 indict optimistic liberalism.

But contemporary Fundamentalism is not without its own moments of guilt. For the world crisis serves to embarrass Fundamentalism also. The uncomfortableness of evangelicalism cannot be palliated by an emphasis on someone else's un-

---

1. The word "humanitarianism" is used in the sense of benevolent regard for the interests of mankind.

easy predicament. Even if it could, the device would hardly escape attention from the alert modern mind.

The predicament of contemporary evangelicalism can be set forth from two vantage points, that of the non-evangelicals and that of the evangelicals themselves. From whichever direction the problem is approached, it is serious enough.

Against Protestant Fundamentalism the non-evangelicals level the charge that it has no social program calling for a practical attack on acknowledged world evils. True, other complaints are made against Christian supernaturalism. Representative spokesmen for religious liberalism, for ethical idealism, for religious humanism, and for pessimism, are linked by a common network of assumptions which clearly differentiates their philosophic premises from the orthodox Hebrew-Christian view. Non-Christian groups have no dealings with a supernaturalistic metaphysics. But nonetheless — though they regard contemporary orthodoxy as a vestigial remnant of traditional obscurantism — they theoretically recognize the philosophic right of the evangelicals to hold any doctrinal framework they may desire. But what is almost wholly unintelligible to the naturalistic and idealistic groups, burdened as they are for a new world order, is the apparent lack of any social passion in Protestant Fundamentalism. On this evaluation, Fundamentalism is the modern priest and Levite, by-passing suffering humanity.

The picture is clear when one brings into focus such admitted social evils as aggressive warfare, racial hatred and intolerance, the liquor traffic, and exploitation of labor or management, whichever it may be.

The social reform movements dedicated to the elimination of such evils do not have the active, let alone vigorous, cooperation of large segments of evangelical Christianity. In fact, Fundamentalist churches increasingly have repudiated the very movements whose most energetic efforts have gone into an attack on such social ills. The studied Fundamentalist avoidance of, and bitter criticism of, the World Council of Churches and the Federal Council of Churches of Christ in America is a pertinent example.

Now, such resistance would be far more intelligible to non-evangelicals were it accompanied by an equally forceful assault on social evils in a distinctly supernaturalistic framework. But, by and large, the Fundamentalist opposition to societal ills has been more vocal than actual. Some concerted effort has been attempted through organizations like the National Association of Evangelicals or the American Council of Churches. Southern Baptists have a somewhat better record, coupled with rejection of the Federal Council. But evangelical social action has been spotty and usually of the emergency type.

The situation has even a darker side. The great majority of Fundamentalist clergymen, during the past generation of world disintegration, became increasingly less vocal about social evils. It was unusual to find a conservative preacher occupied at length with world ills.

In a company of more than one hundred representative evangelical pastors, the writer proposed the following question: "How many of you, during the past six months, have preached a sermon devoted in large part to a condemnation of such social evils as aggressive warfare, racial hatred and intolerance, the liquor traffic, exploitation of labor or management, or the like — a sermon containing not merely an incidental or illustrative reference, but directed mainly against such evils and proposing the framework in which you think solution is possible?" Not a single hand was raised in response. Now this situation is not characteristic only of one particular denominational group of Fundamentalists; rather, a predominant trait, in most Fundamentalist preaching, is this reluctance to come to grips with social evils.

There are Fundamentalist groups, admittedly, which have not lost a keen world reference, especially those alert to their Reformational lineage in John Calvin. Their interest in ethics is demanded, rather than precluded, by their doctrinal fervor. Holding fast to an ideology of supernaturalism, these groups have sometimes been tempted to dissociate themselves from the Fundamentalist camp because of the widespread notion that indifference to world evils is essential to Fundamentalism. And, after all, social irresponsibility was not the only trend that was imputed to Fundamentalist circles. Modern prejudice, justly or unjustly, had come to identify Fundamentalism largely in terms of an anti-ecumenical spirit of independent isolationism, an uncritically-held set of theological formulas,[2] an overly-emotional type of revivalism. There is also the tendency to replace great church music by a barn-dance variety of semi-religious choruses; some churches have almost become spiritualized juke boxes. It was the recognition, by the ethically alert Fundamentalist minority, that such tendencies do not express the inherent genius of the great evangelical tradition that prevented their desertion from the Fundamentalist camp. Spokesmen particularly for orthodox Reformed groups saw that the title of "Fundamentalism" was applied initially with doctrinal fidelity, rather than ethical irresponsibility, as the frame of reference. Fundamentalism was a Bible-believing Christianity which regarded the supernatural as a part of the essence of the Biblical view; the miraculous was not to be

2. Many newspapers have inaccurately applied the Fundamentalist tag to cultists (like the Mormon polygamists) whom the evangelicals would be the first to disown.

viewed, as in liberalism, as an incidental and superfluous accretion. It was from its affirmation of the historic evangelical doctrinal fundamentals that modern orthodoxy received its name, and not from its growing silence on pressing global problems. This was clearly seen by spokesmen for contemporary Fundamentalism like the late J. Gresham Machen, who vigorously insisted that Christianity has a message relevant to the world crisis, however staggering the issues.

The average Fundamentalist's indifference to social implications of his religious message has been so marked, however, that the non-evangelicals have sometimes classified him with the pessimist in his attitude toward world conditions.

Of all the seemingly incongruous weddings in philosophy, this is the most striking. That Christian supernaturalism, which as a matter of historical record furnished the background and in some sense the support for the modern humanisms and idealisms, should be accused of having lost its own devotion to human well-being, is indeed a startling accusation.

But, from the standpoint of not a few religious modernists, ethical idealists and humanists, the common strand that runs through Fundamentalism and pessimism is that both are viewpoints from which the humanism, or humanitarianism, has evaporated.

This is not to suggest that Fundamentalism had no militant opposition to sin. Of all modern viewpoints, when measured against the black background of human nature disclosed by the generation of two world wars, Fundamentalism provided the most realistic appraisal of the condition of man. The sinfulness of man, and the exceeding sinfulness of sin, and that God alone can save man from his disaster, are insistences that were heard with commonplace frequency only within the evangelical churches. But the sin against which Fundamentalism has inveighed, almost exclusively, was individual sin rather than social evil.

It is not fair to say that the ethical platform of all conservative churches has clustered about such platitudes as "abstain from intoxicating beverages, movies, dancing, card-playing, and smoking," but there are multitudes of Fundamentalist congregations in which these are the main points of reference for ethical speculation. In one of the large Christian colleges, a chapel speaker recently expressed amazement that the campus newspaper could devote so much space to the all-important problem of whether it is right to play "rook," while the nations of the world are playing with fire.

And yet it ought not to be overlooked that, in its attack on personal sins, there is an indirect coming to grips in Fundamentalist churches with some of the major contemporary problems. The bitter opposition to intoxicating beverages is, in a localized sense, an attack upon the liquor traffic, even though it does nothing to curb the menace itself and concentrates upon schooling the believer to circumvent it. Again, while the Fundamentalist's opposition to the theatre is sometimes so deep-rooted that it is forgotten that the camera may also serve to the glory of God, he nevertheless is expressing a vigorous protest against the secular and often pagan standards of value which Hollywood film producers have consistently enthroned and glorified. At this point, in fact, the Fundamentalist has often been more sensitive to the danger of undermining Christian convictions by propaganda means than has the religious modernist with his selection of "best, good, and unrecommended films." And yet, the Fundamentalist appears to pursue a rather foredoomed approach, schooling his constituency against all movies, as if they are inherently evil, so that there is no direct attempt to change the external picture itself.

The problem of personal ethics, moreover, is complicated no little by the shifting standards in various sections of the country, among Fundamentalists themselves. Among evangelicals, for example, smoking is hardly considered the sin in the southern tobacco-growing states that it is in the north.[3] And

3. Although the Southern Baptist Convention in 1937 affirmed "that the prevalence of smoking among Christian people, especially among

the northern Baptist pastor who would join his wife for mixed public swimming would be called before his board of deacons in many a southern church.

Now, the purpose of such examples is not to promote a plea for laxity in personal morals. It is simply to emphasize that such personal issues are themselves frequently in a state of environmental flux which, if anything, adds to the predicament of the Fundamentalist pastor on the score of ethical preaching.

Even more serious is the mounting repudiation in evangelical circles of Fundamentalist standards for the practical moral life. This testifies to more than a growing estrangement from traditional ways of living. As seen by those who are not evangelicals, this movement away from the evangelical evaluation of life and duty, in the personal as well as social code of behavior, is an inevitable consequence of an ideology which refuses to relate itself to the cardinal issues of the global dilemma. The non-Christian idealists and naturalists know, of course, that their outlooks demand an evaluation of life which differs from the Fundamental appraisal, but they trace the growing Funda-

---

preachers, church leaders, and denominational workers, is not only detrimental to the health of those who participate, but hurtful to the cause of Christ in that it weakens the messages and lowers the influence of those charged with the preservation and spread of the Gospel."

mentalist revolt against stringent personal prohibitions, to the peculiar strategy of evangelical ethics, as much as to the penetrative dissemination of anti-Christian moral theories. It remains a question whether one can be perpetually indifferent to the problems of social justice and international order, and develop a wholesome personal ethics.

In mentioning the typical ethical insistences of Fundamentalist churches, it would be unfair not to allude to the strict attitude taken toward divorce, as contrasted with the increasingly loose secular view of family relations. The insistence that only death or adultery can sever the marriage bond is maintained nowhere today with such a conviction of absoluteness as in Fundamentalist circles, although there are here, as everywhere, exceptions. The contribution of this viewpoint to the integrity of the family, and its significance in precluding juvenile delinquency, is of no small moment in its social consequences. From a certain perspective it can be said that the effort to remedy the disintegration of the American home, pressed by social reformers, does not get at the heart of the problem as directly as the Fundamentalist proclamation of the divine sanction of a monogamous family life.

But here again it must also be conceded that the defection of American culture from a vital Christianity means that the problem of the home and of juvenile delinquency is unconfronted in countless family circles where remedial measures might create a more favorable soil for the preaching of the Gospel. By such argument even those who have disagreed with a supernaturalist ideology have sought to enlist evangelicalism in reform programs.

The failure of the evangelical movement to react favorably on any widespread front to campaigns against social evils has led, finally, to a suspicion on the part of non-evangelicals that there is something in the very nature of Fundamentalism which makes a world ethical view impossible. The conviction is widespread that Fundamentalism takes too pessimistic a view of human nature to make a social program practicable.

This modern mind-set, insisting that evangelical supernaturalism has inherent within it an ideological fault which precludes any vital social thrust, is one of the most disturbing dividing lines in contemporary thought. In the struggle for a world mind which will make global order and brotherhood a possibility, contemporary speculation has no hearing whatever for a viewpoint which it suspects has no world program. It dismisses Fundamentalism with the thought that, in this expression of the Great Tradition, the humanitarianism has evaporated from Christianity.

CHAPTER II

The Protest Against
Foredoomed Failure

No complaint against Fundamentalism is, from the Fundamentalist viewpoint, more untrue than the contention that the Biblical estimate of man involves a social impotence.

An evangelical message vitally related to world conditions is not precluded by New Testament doctrine.

Indeed, conservative Protestantism insists, *only* this estimate of the sinfulness of man and his need of regeneration is sufficiently realistic to make at all possible any securely-grounded optimism in world affairs. Any other framework can offer only a "bubble and froth cure."

And yet, evangelicalism is disturbed. There is a growing awareness in Fundamentalist circles that, despite the orthodox insistence upon revelation and redemption, evangelical Christianity has become increasingly inarticulate about the social

THE UNEASY CONSCIENCE OF MODERN FUNDAMENTALISM

reference of the Gospel. The conviction mounts that the relationship of the church to world conditions must be reappraised, even if the doctrinal limits are regarded as fixed within which solution is likely to be found. While the modern mind wrestles with its global dilemma, the evangelical conscience is troubled because the historic Christian message is dismissed arbitrarily as a dead option for dissolving the ills of Occidental culture. Fundamentalism is wondering just how it is that a world changing message narrowed its scope to the changing of isolated individuals.

The evangelical predicament is not a simple one.

For one thing, evangelical Christianity views the non-evangelical movements which vigorously promote world social uplift as competitors for the ideological loyalty of the masses. They proclaim rival and contradictory doctrines. The ethical societies, the world brotherhood movements, the united nations organizations, the war prevention agencies — insofar as they seek to attain their ends without an insistence on man's specific need, as a sinner, of individual regeneration — are regarded as hostile to the historic Christian tradition.

This hostility the Fundamentalist refuses to minimize. The whole Biblical viewpoint appears to him at stake. The non-evangelical movements, however desirable their goals, encourage their followers to place their trust in what, from the orthodox viewpoint, is the *wrong method* for attainment of such ends. The Fundamentalist does not think that the ends can be reached by various means, and that his method is better; if he did, the hostility would not be as serious.[1] Rather, the evangelical is convinced that the non-evangelicals operate within the wrong ideological framework to make achievement a possibility. He believes they stimulate a naive and misplaced confidence in man, growing out of a superficial view of reality. He believes the liberal, the humanist, and the ethical idealist share a shallow sense of the depth of world need and an over-optimism concerning man's own supposed resources for far-reaching reversal even of admitted wrongs.

Only an anthropology and a soteriology that insists upon man's sinful lostness and the ability of God to restore the responsive sinner is the adequate key to the door of Fundamentalist world betterment. Any other approach is a needless waste of effort and, in effect an attack on the exclusive relevance, if not on any relevance, of the historic redemptive Gospel. The globe-changing passion of the modern reformers who operate without a Biblical context is, from this vantage point,

---

1. In point of fact, neither do the non-evangelicals think that Fundamentalism is one among many possible methods. The non-evangelicals are in hearty disagreement over the best method; they agree mainly in the conviction that it is not Fundamentalism.

an ignoring of Jesus' insistence that "all these things shall be added" only after man has sought first "the kingdom of God and His righteousness." Non-evangelicals tend to equate the "kingdom" and the "these things," reflecting a blindness to the significance of the vicarious atonement of Christ. The non-evangelicals have a non-evangelical methodology.

Yet the rejection of non-evangelical solutions does not involve — at least, logically — a loss of the social relevance of the Gospel. A globe-changing passion certainly characterized the early church, however much it thought within a redemptive pattern centering in Christ's substitutionary death and bodily resurrection. Had it not been so, Christianity would not have been the religion of the then-known world within three centuries. Some sort of a world passion had made the Christian message pertinent enough for rulers to want to bring their subjects in subjection to it. A Christianity without a passion to turn the world upside down is not reflective of apostolic Christianity.

Consequently, modern Fundamentalism is wondering by what peculiar manipulation of circumstances the Great Tradition has seemingly lost its world relevance. This is doubly marked in our day, when problems often are no longer settled on a community or even national basis except by reference to broader international decisions. For evangelicalism has cautiously avoided any alignment with non-evangelical groups, yet has failed to develop the broad social implications of its message.

The problem is even more complicated for the premillennialist and amillennialist. They are convinced not only that non-evangelicals cannot bring in the perfect social order in their methodological context, but also that the evangelicals will not bring it in by their proclamation of the Gospel. This latter conviction is grounded in the belief that the inauguration of the kingdom awaits the second advent of Christ in His visible return. The amillennialist does not believe in a thousand-year earthly reign, but he shares the despair over the present social order apart from the return of Christ. In this respect, the premillennialists and amillennialists, who together form the largest segment in modern Fundamentalism, are aligned against the postmillennialists, who labor to bring in the kingdom of God by human redemptive effort and anticipate the return of Christ will follow a golden age of world conversion.

It should be emphasized that this despair over the present world order grows, for contemporary Fundamentalism, not out of any lack of confidence in the ability of the supernaturalistic Gospel. Rather, it issues from the fact that the Scriptures, as interpreted by premillenarians and amillenarians, hold forth no hope for the conversion of the whole world, and center upon the second coming of Christ as crucial for the introduction of a divine kingdom. The despair over the present age, then, is grounded in the anticipated lack of response to the redemptive Gospel, rather than in any inherent defect in the message itself.

This Gospel of hope coupled with a prophetic despair has posed, during the past two generations, a problem which Fundamentalism was unable satisfactorily to resolve. Before the rise to power of modern religious liberalism, it was possible for Fundamentalism to proclaim redemptive regeneration as the only solution for world problems, and yet not appear to have lost its social passion. The reason was that most of the creative idealism was within the church itself. But liberalism minimized the necessity of a specifically supernaturalist framework, religious humanism enthroned a thoroughgoing naturalism, and these movements together launched a vigorous attack on great social evils of the modern world.

The recoil of Fundamentalism from such moralism cut loose from Biblical redemption, might have been pursued without a divorce between evangelical doctrinal and evangelical ethical insistence. Historically, Christianity embraced a life view as well as a world view; it was socially as well as philosophically pertinent.

But, almost unawares, Fundamentalism became increasingly absorbed in resistance to non-evangelical humanism as a deceptive competitor for the commitment of multitudes, and because of its prophetic cheerlessness about the present age came more and more to narrow its message for the "faithful remnant" that would be called out of the godless world context. The die was cast, not so much because God had made present world conditions inevitable as because of the foreseen hardness of men's hearts, so that the nonsupernaturalistic idealisms could all be abandoned to future disillusionment. Whereas once the redemptive gospel was a world-changing message, now it was narrowed to a world-resisting message. Out of twentieth century Fundamentalism of this sort there could come no contemporary version of Augustine's *The City of God.*

In protesting against non-evangelical ideologies, Fundamentalism came to react also against the social programs of the modern reformers. This grew in part, as already indicated, out of the conviction that desirable ends were being sought in an undesirable or ineffective context. But, in addition, Fundamentalists came to see that world peace, the brotherhood of man, democracy, and the new economy hardly meant for religious liberalism and humanism what they meant for evangelicalism; that is, Fundamentalism insisted that its ends, as well as its methods, were distinct from the non-evangelical movements. The non-evangelicals were striving for *inadequate ends.*

For example, the non-evangelicals were working for a just
and durable peace which, in theory, was to be achieved by any
possible formula whatever but which, in practice, ruled out
specifically Christian regeneration as its conditioning context.
The end in view was a global peace without any reference to
the vicarious atonement and redemptive work of Christ. To
one who was realistic about human nature, this appeared but a
luxurious dream.

The brotherhood of man, too, had shriveled from New
Testament redemptive proportions. Democracy had meant,
for early Americans, the right to worship God as patterned in
the Scriptures, without the obstruction of earthly powers; between the two world wars it had narrowed down to the four
freedoms, including the right to worship God any way and if
one wanted to do so. That sort of brotherhood, the evangelical
was aware, made brotherhood impossible, because it obscured
man's relationship to God.

The problems of management and labor were now re-
ferred not to a regeneration-conditioned submission to the divine will, but rather to the leftist precepts of political Socialism
or Communism. It was implied in the doctrinal genius of evangelicalism that it must resist such non-evangelical ends, as well
as a non-redemptive methodology. For here existed two defini-
tions of man's true nature and destiny, the one looking for a

perfect material order and the other mainly for a perfect spiritual order.[2]

The reaction against non-evangelical ends manifested itself in a two-fold way, one the way of vocal denunciation and the other the way of silent resistance. The trend toward Communism, as reflected in denominational committees on social action and especially in the Federal Council of Churches, became the topic of vigorous attack. On the other hand, Fundamentalists were quite sure that the disruption of the liquor traffic would hardly put an end to world godlessness, and came to regard the campaign against intoxicants as an inexcusable occupation with a secondary evil; temperance forces sometimes found it harder to present their work in Fundamentalist than in liberal churches. Evangelicalism saw in such moralistic movements the subtle proclamation of a higher, more

2. John C. Bennett discusses the relationship of the liberal Social Gospel to the Christian social imperative and concedes that the Social Gospel "appeared in the context of theological assumptions that were vulnerable and that are now dated" (*Christian Ethics and Social Policy*, p. 2. New York: Charles Scribner's Sons, 1946). But he objects to discarding the term because this "might mean a loss of that vital sense of the social imperative that the Social Gospel means for everyone" (p. 3). The criticisms which a repentant liberalism today makes on the Social Gospel almost invariably are still within a higher liberal framework, making no room for such apostolic doctrines as substitutionary atonement and supernatural regeneration; social sensitivity still runs far deeper than theological sensitivity.

respectable way of life that stood nevertheless at a far remove from the redemptive regeneration of the New Testament, which the church was commissioned to proclaim to the nations. The moralism of pagan idealism was being substituted for the Biblical "good news."

While the non-evangelical groups captured the propaganda centers for their ideology, the evangelicals reacted against the humanistic enthusiasm. The modern reformers in their assaults on aggressive warfare, political statism, racial intolerance, the liquor traffic, labor-management exploitation and other such focal points of tension, had little encouragement from Fundamentalist quarters. Fundamentalism in revolting against the Social Gospel seemed also to revolt against the Christian social imperative.

It was the failure of Fundamentalism to work out a positive message within its own framework, and its tendency instead to take further refuge in a despairing view of world history, that cut off the pertinence of evangelicalism to the modern global crisis. The really creative thought, even if in a non-redemptive context, was now being done by the non-evangelical spokesmen.

The evangelicals were being locked up to the uncomfortable alternative of an attack on contemporary social reformers, seeking solution to admitted ills, or of going along with those whose ideology they did not endorse. Many evangelicals finally were caught up in the social gospel effort, which progressively obscured an evangelical doctrinal context and identified itself correspondingly with ends of the non-evangelical definitional type. But the great majority cut loose deliberately from the social reform movements of the times, denounced as futile and deceptive the world-changing efforts on a non-Biblical formula, and redoubled their efforts to rescue the minority from an increasingly hostile environment.

Now and then came a more visionary Fundamentalist attack on world conditions, predicted on the apostolic passion to change the world by changing the individuals in it. Even the Fundamentalists most interested in prophetic speculations were uneasy over the fact that, however much the early church linked up the consummatory kingdom to the return of Christ, the apostles labored nevertheless with uncompromised passion to carry the Gospel to men everywhere in obedience to the great commission. Spasmodic and isolated efforts were made to link the evangelical message effectively to contemporary world conditions. The uneasy conscience of modern Fundamentalism was stirring. But to become articulate about evangelicalism and its social implications was not an easy task. There is the danger that it might involve an unstudied and superficial analysis of the specific modern evils. For example, one recent Fundamentalist discussion of the social program of the Federal Council of Churches bitterly condemns the Communist leftist trends in that group, while exhibiting a contrasting silence about the evils of a Capitalistic system from which the redemptive reference is largely abstracted.

There is a rising tide of reaction in Fundamentalism today — a reaction born of an uneasy conscience and determined no longer to becloud the challenge of the Gospel to modern times. It is a reaction to which the best minds of evangelicalism are bending their effort these days, convinced that no synthesis is more relevant than modern frustration and Biblical redemptionism.

It was remarked earlier that, during the past two generations, creative ethical thinking was done by those whose ideology was divorced from New Testament supernaturalism, often invading the church itself with the Renaissance humanism of modern philosophy. But that does not necessarily mean truth was on their side. Nothing is clearer today than that the Fundamentalist was dismissed with an almost perverted lightness, when he warned that the non-evangelicals were not delving deeply enough into the nature and destiny of man to prevent a dark disillusionment. After all, the judgment of the two world wars stands now with the appraisal of the Fundamentalist.

The troubled conscience of the modern liberal, growing

out of his superficial optimism, is a deep thing in modern times. But so is the uneasy conscience of the modern Fundamentalist, that no voice is speaking today as Paul would, either at the United Nations sessions, or at labor-management disputes, or in strategic university classrooms whether in Japan or Germany or America.

CHAPTER III

The Most Embarrassing
Evangelical Divorce

For the first protracted period in its history, evangelical Christianity stands divorced from the great social reform movements.

That Christianity has not always been fired by a maximum social passion must be conceded. Despite the fact that the difference between the Oriental and Occidental worlds must be explained to a large extent in terms of Christianity — for the New Testament world-life view lifted the ancient world out of pagan barbarism — it remains true that there have been earlier eras in European history when the church was devoid of measureable social concern. The Roman Catholic Church in the middle ages tended to substitute political for spiritual revolution, and also staunchly supported the feudal system; even today Roman Catholic humanitarianism often appears dictated by expedience, as witness the contrast between Catholic action in Spain, and Latin America, and in the United States. But even in the Lutheran Reformation, Martin Luther too deserted the people in the Peasants' War for social and political improvements which, however much in advance of their day, seem remarkably minimal to us.

But in proportion as the world passion was absent from Christianity, the latter ceased to be an apostolic or missionary Christianity of the type which the Reformation sought to recapture for the western mind. Manifesting its true genius, Christianity furnished an idealistic atmosphere of judgment upon its environment in any age, and precipitated most of the successive reform movements within previous cultures.

However, Fundamentalism today denies that Christian ethics is in any sense to be identified with the humanistic moralism of modern reformers. Yet it is specifically the humanism of the day that is most vocal and vigorous in the attack on admitted social ills. As a consequence, Protestant evangelicalism without a world program has largely relegated itself to a secondary, or even more subordinate, role of challenge to the prevailing cultural mood.[1]

1. John C. Bennett's discussion of the "Four Christian Social Strategies" (i.e., Catholic strategy, the strategy of withdrawal, the identification of Christianity with particular social programs, and the double stan-

One of the ironies of this predicament is that some important benefits have accrued to evangelicals from the very agencies they oppose. A Fundamentalist chaplain recently remarked, for example, that the opportunity to proclaim the evangelical Gospel freely to servicemen had been safe-guarded for him by the influence of the Federal Council of Churches with the national government. He did not mean that the Federal Council had interceded by any means for the historic evangelical message as differentiated from religious modernism, but rather that the whole chaplaincy plan from its inception was closely watched by the Council whereas the evangelicals more or less fell in with it.

Protestantism's embarrassing divorce is apparent. Whereas in previous eras of Occidental history no spiritual force so challenged the human scene as did Christianity with its superlife in the area of conduct, its supernatural world view in the area of philosophy, and its superhope in the area of societal remaking, the challenge of modern Fundamentalism to the

---

dard for personal and public life) is worth reading (*Christian Ethics and Social Policy*, pp. 32 ff). His proposed fifth strategy for relating Christian ethics to social policy falls short to the extent that, while breaking with many of the overoptimistic assumptions of the older Social Gospel, he nonetheless fails properly to relate Christian ethics to the apostolic insistence on individual regeneration through a saving union with the redemptive Christ.

present world mind is almost nonexistent on the great social issues. Through the Christian centuries, assuredly, the evangelical challenge came always in a specifically redemptive framework. But in modern times the challenge is hardly felt at all.[2] For Fundamentalism in the main fails to make relevant to the great moral problems in twentieth-century global living the implications of its redemptive message.

Hebrew-Christian thought, historically, has stood as a closely-knit world and life view. Metaphysics and ethics went everywhere together, in Biblical intent. The great doctrines implied a divinely related social order with intimations for all humanity. The ideal Hebrew or Christian society throbbed with challenge to the predominant culture of its generation, condemning with redemptive might the tolerated social evils, for the redemptive message was to light the world and salt the earth. No insistence on a doctrinal framework alone was sufficient; always this was coupled with the most vigorous assault against evils, so that the globe stood anticipatively at the judgment seat of Christ. Such, at any rate, was apostolic Christian-

2. Many Roman Catholic writers suggest that the Protestant defection from the "universal (Roman) Catholic Church" is the cause of all Protestantism's difficulties. But the Reformation opened the door to a truly spiritual ecumenicity. True, religious modernism precluded an effective realization of that ideal. But it is still a possibility for evangelicalism.

ity; such too was the spirit of the post-apostolic apologies. The emperors must come to terms with Jesus, if not in this life then in the next. If the kingdom of God was not realized on earth, the fault lay not with deity, nor with redemptive metaphysics, but with sinful man.

This theologico-ethical emphasis runs through the Hebrew-Christian outlook. The ultimate values of Biblical supernaturalism are unchanging. New Testament ethics was no more entirely new than New Testament doctrine. The moral, as well as metaphysical, concepts had their Old Testament foregleams, simply because the Biblical view as a whole was rooted in the creative and revelational and regenerative God. In whatever sense the later Christian message did away with the law, it did not set aside any ultimate truths. Both in Old Testament and New Testament thought there is but one sure foundation for a lasting civilization, and its cornerstone is a vital knowledge of the redemptive God. In both eras it is wrong to worship false gods, to murder, to commit adultery, and for a reason more ultimate than that the prophet Moses said so. These deeds were wrong before Moses, yea even before Adam; they have been wrong always, and will be wrong always, because they are antagonistic to the character and will of the sovereign God of the universe. They are wrong for all creatures anywhere anytime. The universe is put together on moral lines; any attempt to build a civilization on other lines, whether before or after the coming of Jesus Christ into the world, foredooms itself. The ten commandments disclose the only secure foundation for a society without the seeds of dissolution; all cultures, cut loose from these principles, have in them the vitiating leaven of decay. And no culture can hope to fulfill such high prerequisites, minus a relationship with that God, holy and redemptive, who is the precondition for their very disclosure to man.

On Old Testament pages no less than New, then, the cardinal doctrines are not divorced from ethical implications. The social outreach of redemptional metaphysics begins for humanity at the very beginnings of the race; Adam implicates all humanity in his fall; the covenant singles out Abraham and his people to bless the world; the Mosaic writings constantly warn that national as well as individual faithfulness to the one true God determines the judgments or blessings of history. One stands with Moses at the close of the Pentateuch, looking prophetically down the corridor of the nation Israel's history, to discover there a philosophy of events with the stamp of eternal validity upon it. The song of Moses, warning of God's judgment while extolling His mercy, is climaxed by counsel to observe "all the words of this law, for it is not a vain thing for you; because it is your life" (Deut. 32:46f). The major as well as minor prophets, lashing out with uncompromised vigor against social evils of the day, breathed the same social passion in a redemption context; the Hebrew world-life view could not look with indifference upon miscarriages of justice in the law courts, usury, plundering the needy, failure to feed and clothe the poor, and over-charging for merchandise.

The New Testament challenge to Greek-Roman culture was an inevitable outcome of the Hebrew-Christian spirit. John the Baptist stood with Moses, Isaiah and Amos in his social alertness. The very words of Isaiah were his rallying point in heralding the coming Redeemer: "The voice of one crying in the wilderness, Prepare ye the way of the Lord . . . all flesh shall see the salvation of God" (Luke 3:4-6). Assuredly, the message of redemption stood at the forefront of the Baptist's preaching. He identifies Jesus to the disciples as "the Lamb of God, which taketh away the sin of the world" (John 1:29), and not to them only, for Jesus' persecutors had "sent unto John, and he bare witness unto the truth" (John 5:33). But the Baptist's redemptive preaching was not on that account socially indifferent. He spoke to a "generation of vipers" (Matt. 3:7) and exhorted, "Repent ye; for the kingdom of heaven is at hand" (Matt. 3:2). He called for "fruits worthy of repentance" (Luke 3:8), declaring that "every tree which bringeth not forth good fruit is hewn down, and cast into the fire" (Luke 3:9). To the specific inquiry,

"What shall we do then?" (Luke 3:10), he gives specific examples. Persons with two coats were to give to those without any. Those with abundant provisions were to share with the needy. Publicans were not to extort. Soldiers were not to commit violence nor accuse individuals falsely. They were probably not to be content with their wages — which was probably not a pronouncement for preservation of the *status quo* in labor management relations, as some humanists insist upon misinterpreting it, but rather a warning against plundering innocent civilians. John's exhortations included "many other things" (Luke 3:18). In fact, his condemnation of adultery in the life of the King led to his own imprisonment and martyrdom: "For John had said unto Herod, It is not lawful for thee to have thy brother's wife" (Mark 6:18).

The social spirit of John's preaching was not contrary to Jesus' own message. Replying to the imprisoned forerunner's inquiry concerning the Christ, Jesus endorses a particular expectation about the Messiah which the Baptist had doubtless gleaned from the Old Testament: "Go and show John again those things which ye do hear and see: the blind receive their sight, and the lame walk, the lepers are cleansed, and the deaf hear, the dead are raised up, and the poor have the gospel preached to them" (Matt. 11:4-5; Luke 7:22). In view of so central a passage, it is difficult to find room for a gospel cut loose entirely from non-spiritual needs. It is true that the New Testament repeatedly employs phrases like the blind seeing, the deaf hearing, and the dead receiving life, in the figurative sense of spiritual regeneration. But that cannot be said for the lame walking, nor for the lepers being cleansed; furthermore, Luke definitely prefixes Jesus' reply to John with the comment that "in the same hour he cured many of their infirmities and plagues, and of evil spirits; and unto many that were blind he gave sight" (7:21). There is no room here for a gospel that is indifferent to the needs of the total man nor of the global man.

Of course, Jesus does not declare that all effort must be bent for world peace; He shares the Biblical conviction that neither peace nor war is as deterministic of human felicity as redemption. Of course He does not declare that there must be a communistic distribution of world goods; He shares the Biblical conviction that redemption is the essential ingredient in the solution of economic problems. Of course He does not declare in formula how a western democracy and a Soviet communist state are to carry on international relations; He shares the Biblical conviction that there is a more relevant need in political science than the intercourse of secularized nations.

But He is not on that account disinterested in the nations and in the global man. One of the blind modern prejudices is our feeling that unless another mind attacks a problem in the way the contemporary mood does, he is not interested in it. The methodology of Jesus is a redemption methodology, and the modern formulas have been so different simply because of their presupposition that redemption is an alien concept for the contemporary world. But there is not a problem of global consequence but that, from the viewpoint of Jesus, redemption is a relevant formula. It is offered as the only adequate rest for world weariness, whether political, economic, academic, recreational. It stands in judgment upon all non-Christian solutions.

Paul's position likewise involves an ethical universalism, for he is concerned with more than individual morals. The gospel of Christ cuts across all human distinctions, and He is the lone Lord of humanity, with the only adequate relief for man's needs. The apostle to the Gentiles thus proclaims a social, as well as personal, Christianity. His missionary passion contradicts any view that he conceived of the believer's life as an exclusive privilege to be lived in monastic privacy; rather, he was spiritually aflame to bring the world to the feet of Jesus.

This early outlook, seeking to relate Christianity redemptively to the Graeco-Roman environment of the day, so characterized the apostolic witness that within three centuries the new religion had, in large measure, captured the then-known world. Whatever their view of the kingdom, the early Christians did not permit it to interfere with their world-changing zeal; they were not embarrassed that some opponents should suspect them of turning the world "upside down." This does not mean that early Christianity charted the course for social reform; rather, it furnished the basic principles and the moral dynamic for such reform, and concentrated on regeneration as the guarantee of bettered conditions.[3]

It is not denied, of course, that Roman Catholic imperialism soon substituted political aggrandizement for spiritual regeneration; the so-called Christian culture of the middle ages tended rather to be an outwardly ritualized form of Graeco-Roman culture, although the impact of the Christian witness could not be totally lost. In other spotty areas of church history, there appeared an emphasis on the other-worldliness of Christianity, as in the monastic movements. Thomas a Kempis' *The Imitation of Christ* may be a later expression of this

3. There is renewed appreciation today of the fact that a message which concentrates on individual regeneration may be on that very account socially relevant rather than socially irrelevant. The higher liberals learned many lessons from the war years 1914-46. Ernest F. Scott now reminds us that "Jesus' one remedy for social abuses is the renewal of the individual will. If men become different in their own hearts their actions will be different, and the outcome will be a new society, in which there will be right relations between man and man" (*Man and Society in the New Testament*, p. 197. New York: Charles Scribner's Sons, 1946).

mood, though he may be explicating not fundamental motives as much as personal morality.

Yet the early patriotic moralists attacked pagan ethical standards — idolatry, sensuous luxury, sexual looseness, theatrical obscenity, gladiatorial cruelties, infanticide and abortion, commercial deceit; everywhere they pitched the Christian message against social immoralities. Augustine's *City of God* insisted that the temporal and eternal cities exist concurrently in history, as against the view that the kingdom of God is to be identified with super-history alone. When Aquinas formulated in the thirteenth century the theological system which still is the frame of reference for Roman Catholic divinity, a detailed study of Christian ethics both social and personal was an essential part of his task.

Much of the blame for the early Renaissance interest in social theory must be attributed to the corruption within the Roman Catholic church, which led ultimately to the Reformational revolt. Martin Luther, the father of the Reformation, hurled his full weight against the medieval concept of a works-salvation, but the ethical implications of his Gospel message were not wrought out with complete satisfaction. Luther bemoaned the moral deterioration of his day, but he placed an underemphasis on sanctification in his teaching and example, and his conduct in the Peasants' War is not a happy chapter in the story of the Reformation. The Zwinglian Reformation in Switzerland, however, became more articulate about the civil and moral implications of regeneration, and the Calvinistic Reformation moved toward a truly catholic view of the Christian life. Calvin felt that the Hebrew-Christian tradition historically involved an articulate statement not only of dogmatics but of the social implications of redemption.

Today, Protestant Fundamentalism although heir-apparent to the supernaturalist gospel of the Biblical and Reformation minds, is a stranger, in its predominant spirit, to the vigorous social interest of its ideological forebears. Modern Fundamentalism does not explicitly sketch the social implications of its message for the non-Christian world; it does not challenge the injustices of the totalitarianisms, the secularisms of modern education, the evils of racial hatred, the wrongs of current labor-management relations, the inadequate bases of international dealings. It has ceased to challenge Caesar and Rome, as though in futile resignation and submission to the triumphant Renaissance mood. The apostolic Gospel stands divorced from a passion to right the world. The Christian social imperative is today in the hands of those who understand it in sub-Christian terms.

But evangelicalism is disturbed proportionately as it senses this contradiction of its own history. Fundamentalism is agitating today with two great convictions, the affirmation of which is necessary if Fundamentalism is to express the genius of the Christian tradition: (1) That Christianity opposes any and every evil, personal and social, and must never be represented as in any way tolerant of such evil; (2) That Christianity opposes to such evil, as the only sufficient formula for its resolution, the redemptive work of Jesus Christ and the regenerative work of the Holy Spirit. It rejects the charge that the Fundamentalist ideology logically involves an indifference to social evils, and presses the contention that the non-evangelical ideology involves an essential inability to right the world order. It is discerning anew that an assault on global evils is not only consistent with, but rather is demanded by, its proper world-life view.

CHAPTER IV

The Apprehension Over Kingdom Preaching

There has been more millennial fanaticism in modern anti-supernaturalistic theories than in contemporary evangelicalism. One of the curiosities of church history is that the naturalistic world-view, so hostile to the Christian notion of the kingdom, finally embraced zealously the idea of an immanent millennium.[1]

The millennial enthusiasm or "carnal chiliasm" of Münzer and the Zwickau prophets and of Matthys and the Münster

---

1. Herbert Spencer was an apostle of such optimism: "The inference that as advancement has been hitherto the rule, it will be the rule henceforth, may be called a plausible speculation. But when it is shown that this advancement is due to the working of a universal law; and that in virtue of that law it must continue until the state we call perfection is reached, then the belief in that state is removed out of the region of probability into that of certainty (*Social Statistics*, p. 78. New York: D. Appleton and Co., 1883).

kingdom, is not representative of modern Fundamentalism. In non-dispensational Fundamentalism, amillennialists and premillennialists agree that the kingdom whether earthly or heavenly will be set up not by the flashed sword of Gideon but by the advent of Christ, though a real spiritual reign is insisted upon in Christ's present relationship to the church. In dispensational Fundamentalism, the keynote of the postponement theory is "no kingdom now, but rather a future kingdom." Therefore modern Fundamentalism has not shared the sentiment for an immediate and forced bringing in of the kingdom. That mood, rather, characterized modern liberalism, with its strategy for abolishing social inequities; kingdom fanaticism had found, in recent times, a strange bedfellow indeed.

Nevertheless, Fundamentalism steadfastly proclaimed the future kingdom as a certainty, for the triumph of righteousness was inevitable in a moral universe. The postmillennial optimism that the kingdom was to be ushered in by the effort of believers prior to the return of Christ, was largely compromised by the first World War. Even previous to that time, however, cautious evangelicals like James Orr tempered their postmillennial optimism with the conviction that the final thrust in establishing the kingdom would require the advent of Christ.[2] In the

2. On this view, utopianism could be safeguarded against relapse only by the presence of the King.

aftermath of the second World War, evangelical postmillennialism almost wholly abandoned the field of kingdom preaching to premillennialism and amillennialism, united in the common conviction that the return of Christ is a prerequisite for the future golden age, but divided over whether it will involve an earthly millennium. Assured of the ultimate triumph of right, contemporary evangelicalism avoids a minimizing of earthly hostility to the gospel, as well as rejects the naturalistic optimism centering in evolutionary automatic progress. The bright hope of the immanent return of Christ is not minimized, and the kingdom hope is clearly distinguishable from the liberal confidence in a new social order of human making only.

Recent Fundamentalism increasingly reflects a marked hesitancy about kingdom preaching.

The tendency to identify the kingdom with any present earthly social order, however modified in a democratic or communistic direction, always has been resisted by evangelicals. As against secular humanism, Fundamentalism has consistently witnessed to the fact that any culture from which the redemptive element is absent is essentially distinct from the kingdom of God. It is this concept of supernatural redemption that furnishes the unique ingredient of the divine kingdom. Cultures which tend to be democratic rather than totalitarian may be preferential for many reasons, but they are not, therefore, to be equated with the kingdom. For this reason, Fundamentalism has resisted the *kingdom now* mood which characterized much liberal preaching.

On the other hand, Fundamentalism also discloses an apprehension over *kingdom then* preaching. This is partly due to prophetic extravagances which the second World War repudiated, though Fundamentalist excesses on this score hardly suffered as rudely as did the liberal optimism about the future. Nevertheless, the prophetic movement had numerous embarrassing elements. It was not only that dogmatic predictions, such as that concerning a revived Roman empire, sorely miscarried, though prophetic disillusionment was serious enough. For the tendency personally to identify an anti-Christ, the division of evangelicals not only over the millennial question but over such problems as the pre-tribulation, mid-tribulation or post-tribulation rapture, concentrated the emphasis on Fundamentalist differences rather than on the basic supernaturalistic ideology which they unitedly opposed to the prevailing empirical-naturalistic worldview. But even more serious was the fact that some Fundamentalist workers substituted a familiarity with the prophetic teaching of the Bible for an aggressive effort to proclaim Christ as the potent answer to the dissolution of world culture. As a consequence, they trained enlightened spectators, rather than empowered ambassadors. Prophetic conference, rather than pentecostal challenge, was their forte.

These factors have engendered a reaction involving the *kingdom then* message. Some responsible Fundamentalists have acknowledged unjustifiable inferences in their pre-war prophetic utterances. This does not involve, by any means, their error at all points. The humanists and modernists who are unmoved by fulfilled predictions such as a Palestine rejuvenated by the immigration of non-Christian Jews, must come to terms at all events with the fulfillment of Fundamentalist insistence that world events would wax worse rather than better. Nevertheless there has been sufficient basis for a frank confession of prophetic extravagance.

Furthermore, there is a noticeable shift in eschatological thinking. On the one hand, there appears a return to a more conservative type of premillennialism, such as that of Alford and Trench, with an accompanying tendency to discard dogmatism on details; if this continues, the eschatological preaching of next generation Fundamentalists will concentrate on the proclamation of the kingdom, the second coming, the bodily resurrection of the dead, and the future judgment, and will not concern itself too much with lesser events. On the other hand, some evangelicals revolting against the prophetic detail of dispensational premillennialism, are discarding premillennialism along with the detail, and shifting toward an amillennial position. It is not within the province of this study to set forth arguments for or against such a trend. The writer's own convictions are broadly premillennial, and he is not convinced that a discard of speculative accretions justifies an uncritical surrender of the whole premillennial structure; if the shift to amillennial grounds is made on firmer convictions, that is a different matter. But it is within the province of this volume to urge upon evangelicals the necessity for a deliberate restudy of the whole kingdom question, that the great evangelical agreements may be set effectively over against the modern mind, with the least dissipation of energy on secondary issues.

The writer was cautioned by a Fundamentalist spokesman, when this series of articles was projected, to "stay away from the kingdom." There is growing reluctance to explicate the kingdom idea in Fundamentalist preaching, because a *kingdom now* message is too easily confused with the liberal social gospel, and because a *kingdom then* message will identify Christianity further to the modern mind in terms of an escape mechanism.

Yet no subject was more frequently on the lips of Jesus Christ than the kingdom. He proclaimed kingdom truth with a constant, exuberant joy. It appears as the central theme of His preaching. To delete His kingdom references, parabolic and nonparabolic, would be to excise most of His words. The concept "kingdom of God" or "kingdom of heaven" is heard repeatedly from His lips, and it colors all of His works.

It is not purposed here to project any new kingdom theory; exegetical novelty so late in church history may well be suspect. Nor is it purposed to evaluate in detail the prevailing theories: that cannot be done competently in such brief compass. The writer's own convictions, while broadly premillennial, are not partial to the dispensational postponement theory of the kingdom; this is no necessary adjunct of the premillennial view. It appears more in accord with the Biblical philosophy of history to think of the church age in terms of divine continuity rather than of parenthesis, in terms of the amazing unity of the redemptive plan rather than in terms of an amazing interlude.[3] The writer feels that the prophecies demand a future earthly

---

3. According to the postponement theory, Jesus was to set up the Davidic kingdom at His first coming but, due to His rejection, the "mystery form" of the kingdom was introduced. As a consequence, the divine plan during this church age is concerned, it is said, only with "calling out" believers. This theory has gained wide support in the north during the past two generations; many persons automatically identify if not only with all premillennialism, but with all Fundamentalism. Johannes Weiss, Albert Schweitzer and others of the so-called "consistent school of eschatology" contend that Jesus, viewed as a gifted human prophet merely, preached *only* a future eschatological kingdom — a view which has remote affinities to the postponement theory with its one-sided futurist emphasis, though of course there is here no thought of any offer of the kingdom to the Jews.

kingdom, and are not fully exhausted by the idea of an eternal spiritual kingdom.[4] Nevertheless, the burden of these articles is not to press a personal kingdom viewpoint, but rather to promote an evangelical conviction that nothing is so essential among Fundamentalist essentials as a world-relevance for the Gospel. Whatever in our kingdom views undercuts that relevance destroys the essential character of Christianity as such.

No study of the kingdom teaching of Jesus is adequate unless it recognizes His implication both that the kingdom is here, and that it is not here.[5] This does not imply an ultimate paradox, but rather stresses that the kingdom exists in incomplete realization. The task of the Bible student is to discover (1) in what sense it is here; (2) in what sense it is to be further realized before the advent of Christ; and (3) in what sense it will be fully realized at the advent of Christ.

---

4. James Orr expressed this sentiment in a delightful manner: "But this I would confess, that the idea of a latter day of glory on this earth of ours — a period of Sabbath rest and realization of righteousness — has a charm to my mind, and seems to me to have its roots in so much Old Testament prediction, that I cannot willingly forego it . . ." (*Sidelights on Christian Doctrine*, p. 174).

5. F. J. Foakes-Jackson and Kirsopp Lake insisted that the kingdom of God in the Gospels has a two-fold reference: it is a future kingdom, proclaimed as at hand; it is a present kingdom in the sovereignty of God. "All attempts . . . to explain these two meanings of the kingdom of God by eliminating one of them have failed" (*The Beginnings of Christianity*, I, p. 280).

Matthew's Gospel, deliberately stressing the continuity between the Old Testament prophecies and their Messianic fulfillment in Jesus Christ, is the most Jewish of the Gospels. Here, if anywhere, one should find a clear indication of the meaning of the kingdom idea in the teaching of Jesus.

Jesus obviously did not usher in an earthly political kingdom at His coming. Further, He did not attempt to do so only to abandon the idea. The disciples did not go forth to overthrow the Roman empire by force of arms. Nor did Caesar come into necessary conflict with the kingdom idea; such conflict would ensue only when Caesar demanded what was God's due. The kingdom which Jesus introduced, it appears, was quite compatible with earthly government which did not interfere with the realization of the *summum bonum* in the lives of regenerate believers, but it could hardly be identified with any government in which the redemptive reference was not central. The main difference between the kingdom of God *now* and the kingdom of God *then* is that the future kingdom will center all of its activities in the redemptive King because all government and dominion will be subjected to Him. This difference overshadows the question, however important, whether the future kingdom involves an earthly reign or not.

The extent to which man centers his life and energy in the redemptive King *now* determines the extent of the divine king-

dom in the present age. That kingdom is not to be totally identified with any earthly rule, though some have subserved and
others have opposed the redemptive program. Human government need not conflict with divine government unless it so
decrees and, if it does, the kingdom of God secures its ends primarily by spiritual rather than political revolution; eventually,
however, because this is a moral universe and the inevitable
wages of sin is death, the divine victory is won in both areas.
Graeco-Roman culture fell before the medieval mind not because Jesus sought to pressure the Jewish government into line
with His principles, nor because the disciples endeavored to
destroy the Roman empire. Neither the fall of Herod's throne
nor the overthrow of Caesar was an announced prerequisite
for the *at handness* of the kingdom of God. That kingdom was a
spiritual relationship of individuals to Jesus Christ as their redemptive King. It did not await the overthrow, or establishment, of any specified type of earthly political government;
presumably it was compatible with any earthly rule that did no
violence to the redemptive reference. A totalitarianism without such violence would be better than a democracy with it,
and vice versa. But even then, a totalitarianism or a democracy
with such a reference would not on that account be identified
with the kingdom of God in its totality, for in the *then* kingdom
all life and activity will have a redemptive center.

In the establishment of the *now* kingdom, the Gospel of Jesus does not ride rough shod in political power over the oppositions of men; in the establishment of the *then* kingdom, there will be evident a fiery and cataclysmic consummation. By true instinct the Christian church has prayed through the ages, after the Redeemer: "Thy kingdom come; Thy will be done on earth as it is in heaven." The Hebrew parallelism of this prayer declares how wide is the gap between the *new* kingdom and the *then* kingdom.

The apostolic view of the kingdom should likewise be definitive for contemporary evangelicalism. There does not seem much apostolic apprehension over kingdom preaching. We read that Philip preached "good news about the kingdom of God and the name of Jesus Christ" (Acts 8:12). Paul in the Ephesus synagogue boldly argued and pleaded "about the kingdom of God" (Acts 19:8), and identified the Ephesian elders in his farewell address as those "among whom I have gone about preaching the kingdom" (Acts 20:25). Arriving in Rome, Paul testified "to the kingdom of God, trying to convince them about Jesus both from the law of Moses and from the prophets" (Acts 28:23). For two years he lived in that city, "preaching the kingdom of God and teaching about the Lord Jesus Christ" (Acts 28-31).

The apostolic notion of the kingdom is characterized by

the same *now* and *then* aspects discoverable in the teaching of
Jesus.

The kingdom is not wholly future. Paul writes the Romans
that the kingdom of God means "righteousness and peace and
joy in the Holy Spirit" (Rom. 14:17). He writes the Corinthians
that the kingdom of God "does not consist in talk but in
power" (1 Cor. 4:20). He writes the Colossians that the Father
"has transferred us to the kingdom of his beloved Son, in
whom we have redemption, the forgiveness of sins" (Col. 1:13).
The author of the epistle to the Hebrews writes: "Let us be
grateful for receiving a kingdom that cannot be shaken, and let
us offer to God acceptable worship, with reverence and awe"
(Heb. 12:28). The Apocalypst writes: "I John, your brother, who
share with you in Jesus the tribulation and the kingdom and
the patient endurance . . ." (Rev. 1:9). These passages, among
others, argue clearly that the kingdom is a present spiritual reality in the lives of believers, being coextensive with the out-
worked redemptive and regenerative plan of God.

Yet the kingdom has a glorious future aspect. Paul writes
the Corinthians that the coming of Christ and the resurrection
of the righteous dead precedes the end-time "when Christ de-
livers the kingdom to God the Father after destroying every
rule and every authority and power" (1 Cor. 15:24). Quite
clearly, the reign of Christ involves an era when all His enemies

are not underfoot, and an era when they are. Again, Paul writes that "flesh and blood cannot inherit the kingdom of God" (1 Cor. 15:50), explaining that perishable things cannot inherit the imperishable. He charges Timothy "in the presence of God and of Christ Jesus who is to judge the living and the dead, at his appearing and at his kingdom" (2 Tim. 4:1), and adds, "The Lord will rescue me from every evil and save me for his heavenly kingdom" (2 Tim. 4:18). Peter urges the brethren to "confirm your call and election . . . so there will be richly provided for you an entrance into the eternal kingdom of our Lord and Saviour Jesus Christ" (2 Peter 1:10-11). The Apocalyptist looks ahead to the day when "the kingdom of the world has become the kingdom of our Lord and of his Christ, and he shall reign forever and ever" (Rev. 11:15), and to the day when "the salvation and the power and the kingdom of our God and the authority of His Christ have come" (Rev. 12:10). The disciples too, after the crucifixion and resurrection of Jesus, hear His instruction concerning the kingdom of God, and inquire when the kingdom will be restored to Israel (Acts 1:6). The present spiritual kingdom constituted by the reign of Christ in the hearts of believers clearly does not exhaust the declarations concerning a future kingdom, when every opposing or resisting power shall be subjected to Christ.

Contemporary evangelicalism needs (1) to reawaken to the

relevance of its redemptive message to the global predicament; (2) to stress the great evangelical agreements in a common world front; (3) to discard elements of its message which cut the nerve of world compassion as contradictory to the inherent genius of Christianity; (4) to restudy eschatological convictions for a proper perspective which will not unnecessarily dissipate evangelical strength in controversy over secondary positions, in a day when the significance of the primary insistences is international.

CHAPTER V

The Fundamentalist Thief on the Cross

The two thieves between whom Jesus was crucified might, without too wild an imagination, bear the labels of humanism and Fundamentalism. The one on the left felt that Jesus had no momentous contribution to suffering humanity, while the one on the right was convinced of His saviourhood but wanted to be remembered in the indefinite future, when Jesus would come into His kingdom.

Contemporary Fundamentalism needs to meditate long hours on the Saviour's reply: "*Today* shalt thou be with me in paradise." The message for decadent modern civilization must ring with the present tense. We must confront the world *now* with an ethics to make it tremble, and with a dynamic to give it hope.

It is quite popular at the moment to crucify the Fundamentalist. That is not the object of this series of articles; there is no sympathy here for the distorted attack on Fundamentalism so often pressed by liberals and humanists. To conceal his own embarrassment, many a liberal today follows a planned strategy of thanking God he is not a Fundamentalist. A frequent pattern is to remark that of course the liberal repudiates the obscurantism of taking the whole Bible literally, or of thinking God dictated it without respecting the personalities of the writers, or of contending that God stopped working in human history 1900 years ago. What is not remarked is that no representative Fundamentalist thinks that either. But, by the device of differentiating liberalism from a position so extreme that only a mental incompetent would subscribe to it, the sting is supposedly removed from liberalism's death. The Fundamentalist is placed on the cross, while the liberal goes scot free in a forest of weasel words.

The intent of these articles, on the other hand, is to show that viewpoints identified with Fundamentalism have a right to that claim only as they share the historic doctrines and the historic superlife. Part of that superlife is a passion to bring men everywhere to a knowledge of Jesus Christ. A Fundamentalism from which such a passion is absent becomes an inessentialism. Here, if anywhere, the test of "negative pragmatism,"[1] appears appropriate indeed. If Fundamentalism ceases to "work," we have imported into it elements which violate the innermost essence of Christianity. The apostles were convinced not only that they possessed the one name under heaven whereby men must be saved, but also that they were the ambassadors for Christ whose faithful service measured the impact of redemptionism upon their generation. This volume covets for the whole evangelical movement a new life and vigor on the destitute world front.

The supernaturalist framework of historic Christianity is here espoused as the lone solution of modern dilemmas. That solution is not the renunciation of naturalism in the name of Platonic idealism, nor Kierkegaardian existentialism, but the reaffirmation of Hebrew-Christian redemptionism. When classic Fundamentalism is properly differentiated from other views, the stress does not fall on excesses or accretions unacceptable to the evangelical mind as a whole. The true differentia come into vital conflict with the controversial issues in modern thought. Fundamentalism insists upon a purposive and moral as over against a purely mathematical uni-

---

1. Pragmatism affirms that a thing is true because it works: Christianity rather that it works because it is true. Negative pragmatism — as Hocking set it forth — affirms merely that unless it works, it cannot be true.

verse; it insists upon a personal God, as against impersonal ultimates whether of the space-time or *élan vital* variety; it insists upon a divine creation as over against a naturalistic evolution; it insists that man's uniqueness is a divine endowment rather than a human achievement; it insists that man's predicament is not an animal inheritance nor a necessity of his nature but rather a consequence of his voluntary revolt against God; it insists that salvation can be provided only by God, as against the view that man is competent to save himself; it insists that the Scriptures are a revelation lighting the way to the divine incarnation in Jesus Christ as the Redeemer of mankind, as against the view that they stand among many records of religious experience without a difference in kind; it insists that history is bound up with man's acceptance or rejection of the God-man, rather than that history is primarily what happens among nations; it insists that the future is not an open question, but that world events move toward an ultimate consummation in a future judgment of the race.

One needs to view Fundamentalism in this perspective before it is apparent how distorted is any identification in terms of eschatology only. There are, no doubt, Fundamentalists who do not express the true genius of Fundamentalism any more than some so-called Hegelians or Kantians are representative of the philosophers whose names they bear. There is no necessity for abandonment of the Fundamentalist fort, on such secondary grounds, nor for moving to an obscure neo-Fundamentalist position, or to so-called conservatism as differentiated from Fundamentalism; there is already too much terminological confusion, and one always runs the danger of being identified with liberal Fundamentalists who emphasize only the fundamentals of liberalism, and the further danger of encouraging a willingness to be misunderstood.

The revitalization of modern evangelicalism will not come by a discard of its doctrinal convictions and a movement in the direction of liberalism. For current history has decisively unmasked liberal unrealism. Precisely those non-evangelical ideologies which prevailed during the past generation have ended in frustration. They have not averted the most serious debacle in history, after displacing Christian supernaturalism on the questionable ground that it had not worked in earlier ages; the judgment of history, by clearer perspective than ours, will discern how directly such ideologies contributed to that debacle by undercutting supernatural sanctions.

The evangelical may often believe too much, but the sweep of his ideology at least includes the great essentials. The time has come now for Fundamentalism to speak with an ecumenical outlook and voice; if it speaks in terms of the historic Biblical tradition, rather than in the name of secondary accretions or of eschatological biases on which evangelicals divide, it can refashion the modern mind. But a double-minded Fundamentalism — which veers between essentials and inessentials — will receive little of the Lord, and not much of a hearing from the perishing multitudes.

The author's Reformed friends insist that Fundamentalism needs to incorporate into its doctrine a view of common grace, thus securing a vital philosophy of history. His amillennial friends insist that amillennialism is the neglected key; his premillennial friends terms this a shallow solution. Others suggest that the biggest evangelical need is a spiritual revival to sweep away what Dr. William Ward Ayer terms "pharisaical fundamentalism," applied to those — fortunately not numerous — who are doctrinally sound but ethically unsound. Dr. Ayer deplores the "pharisaical spirit of fundamentalism" and warns that "unless there is a resurgence of love, power and breadth of mind and spirit in our midst we shall more effectively deny the faith than the religiously-shallow modernists can ever do. Their following is limited; ours is large." Others hold that the basic need is for a common determination to concentrate on those great doctrines which can steer the modern mind aright at the points of severest tension.

The evangelical uneasiness is one of the most promising signs of the times, for it may issue in a formula providing a twentieth-century reformation within Protestantism and leading to a global renaissance within modern secularism. Evangelicalism already has the advantage of agreement on great doctrines, whereas no contemporary ideology can claim such great numbers who stand united on so wide a front. Liberalism is caught in transition, with little agreement. It swings indecisively between the notion of a personal God and a creative force for which the term "personal" may be a symbol; it swings inconsistently between acceptance of the tentativity of the scientific method and the claim that Jesus has an absolute meaning for history; it fluctuates uncertainly between its former view that man is essentially good and a view that man is somehow essentially bad, and when it adopts the latter it robs sin of its true character as sin. But Fundamentalism is agreed on the main doctrines of God, of creation, of anthropology, of soteriology, and of eschatology in its main peaks. It was great doctrine, centering in the Living Christ as Redeemer, that the early church proclaimed to the dying culture of its day.

To engage the time of the contemporary mind at secondary points is to miss our opportunity, for the main tenets of Biblical supernaturalism are most relevant to the modern tensions. The central affirmations of the Hebrew-Christian message need most to be heard. The hour now is so desperate that the Biblical view will strike upon modern indecision with a power directly proportionate to the immediacy or delay in its proclamation.

The evangelical answer is to be presented not primarily as a rejected opportunity, though it has been that through the centuries in differing measures, but as a present solution, if only men and nations will come to terms with Jesus. That they must come to terms with Him later is always a timely insistence, but not as timely right now as the emphasis that God works in history as well as in superhistory.

Perhaps this picture of Jesus standing at the tomb of our disintegrating renaissance culture can be emphasized by an allegory built on the raising of Lazarus. When death overtook Lazarus, and plunged his survivors into grief, Jesus came with assurance that "thy brother shall rise again." Martha replied, "I know that he shall rise again *in the resurrection at the last day*" (John 11:24). Such Fundamentalism as reduces God's role in history largely to a preparation for future judgment may well pause at the tomb of Lazarus. There Jesus cried out, "I *am* the resurrection and the life . . . Lazarus, come forth!"

The problem of Fundamentalism then is basically not one of finding a valid message, but rather of giving the redemptive word a proper temporal focus. Christianity still affords the supreme dynamic, the supreme world-view, the supreme hope; wherever men tend to rest with a lesser dynamic, with a sub-

Christian philosophy, and with a lesser hope, it is and always will be pertinent.

If Protestant orthodoxy holds itself aloof from the present world predicament it is doomed to a much reduced role; in the previous crises of culture, whether the challenge of the Graeco-Roman world in the apostolic age, or the challenge of a corrupt medieval Catholicism in the Reformation movement, orthodoxy led the battle for a new order, and was not content with a secondary or tertiary role. If the evangelical answer is in terms of religious escapism, then the salt has lost its savor.

Our obligation to speak is not lessened by our conviction of the immanent return of Christ. What if we rise tomorrow? — we are *here* today, and a global mission field is here with us.

CHAPTER VI

The Struggle for a
New World Mind

If historic Christianity is again to compete as a vital world ideology, evangelicalism must project a solution for the most pressing world problems. It must offer a formula for a new world mind with spiritual ends,[1] involving evangelical affirmations in political, economic, sociological, and educational realms, local and international. The redemptive message has implications for all of life; a truncated life results from a truncated message.

Evangelicalism may never succeed, on the missionary approach, in remaking the modern mind in such a way that the future world culture can be identified fully as a Christian civilization. In order to become globally vigorous, Fundamentalism

1. See the author's *Remaking the Modern Mind* (Grand Rapids: Wm. B. Eerdmans Publ. Co., 1946).

need not share the dream, now being discarded by liberalism, of an immanent utopia; an adequate insight both into human nature and into New Testament truth furnishes good ground for doubt that the kingdom can be established without the advent of Christ.

But Fundamentalism does not share the recent tendency, found both in neo-supernaturalist and higher liberal circles, to view man as a sinner by an ultimate necessity of his nature, as though he were destined originally to contradiction and failure. The evangelical and non-evangelical views grow, at this point, out of differing attitudes toward primal anthropology. The Fundamentalist holds that primal man was a divine creation, endowed with moral righteousness, so that man is not a sinner by a necessity of his original nature, but rather by voluntary choice; consequently, the hope for a better order is directly proportionate to the appropriation of redemptive grace in human society. The neo-supernaturalists and liberals adopt the evolutionary view of origins, and discard any notion of a fall from primal perfection involving man in original sin. Man's imperfection, on this approach, is identified with inherited brute instincts or the limitations of his nature as a man; the hope for a better order, on this view, is directly proportionate to his success in affirming a higher self as against his natural self, with a bias in the direction of failure. In the light of the two world wars, liberalism thus discards its faith in automatic progress which formerly characterized the social gospel; we are now told by Paul Tillich, for example, that "the authentic Christian message is never utopian."[2] Evangelicalism does not believe that man's progress is limited by man's nature as man, as much as by his refusal to appropriate divine regenerative grace.

Therefore evangelicalism can view the future with a sober optimism, grounded not only in the assurance of the ultimate triumph of righteousness, but also in the conviction that divine redemption can be a potent factor in any age. That evangelicalism may not create a fully Christian civilization does not argue against an effort to win as many areas as possible by the redemptive power of Christ; it can engender reformation here, and overthrow paganism there; it can win outlets for the redemption that is in Christ Jesus reminiscent of apostolic triumphs. If Christianity cannot bring new life to Russia, that is no argument for not bringing it to China; if it cannot bring reformation to Spain, that is no reason for not bringing it to South America. A single voice that speaks for Jesus in our global conferences can be a determinative voice. The world has awakened suddenly to the astonishing potentiality of an

2. Van Dusen, Henry P. (Editor), *The Christian Answer*, p. 44 (New York: Charles Scribner's Sons, 1945).

individual veto. It is apparent how great nations are keyed to powerful leaders; a single statesman with the convictions of Paul would echo the great evangelical affirmations throughout world politics.

Evangelicalism will have to contend for a new order in education. The western concept of popular education has its legitimate rootage in the determination of the church to indoctrinate the masses in the major doctrinal essentials of the Christian world-life view. For the past three centuries, the state has steadily supplanted the church as the indoctrinating agency, and today secular education largely involves an open or subtle undermining of historic Christian theism.

Evangelicalism must contend, under such circumstances, for two great academic changes.

First, it must develop a competent literature in every field of study, on every level from the grade school through the university, which adequately presents each subject with its implications from the Christian as well as non-Christian points of view. The bias and prejudice to which modern secularism yielded, in the very name of a revolt against dogmatism and in the supposed interest of impartiality, is becoming increasingly obvious to anyone familiar with the modern mood. Evangelicalism must contend for a fair hearing for the Christian mind, among other minds, in secular education. Almost every philo-

plan may be appropriate. From an investment standpoint, the average evangelical church building has many disadvantages.

The day has now come for evangelicalism to rethink its whole building program. By tremendous outlay of funds, most church communities provide a worship structure which usually stands idle except for two Sunday services and a midweek prayer meeting, if the latter. No secular steward could long be happy about such a minimal use of facilities representing so disproportionate an investment. Out of the modern crisis may come a better stewardship. Perhaps the answer is the building of evangelical educational plants, with attractive auditoriums that will serve for worship purposes, providing a week-round program that out-educates the secular educators. The fact that Christian teachers are not over-numerous further attests the need for such a program. Beyond doubt the time is here for an all-out evangelical education movement, and alert churches will think through the wise investment of their funds. The maintenance of evangelical grade and high schools, and of evangelical colleges and universities, with the highest academic standards, promises most quickly to concentrate the thinking of youth upon the Christian world-life view as the only adequate spiritual ground for a surviving culture. A huge share of the gifts which made possible the present secular colleges and universities of America came in the first place from evangelicals with just such a vision; it remains for evangelicalism, despite the encrustations of modernism and humanism, to fulfill that vision. If it entails sacrifice, it will not on that account be displeasing to Jesus Christ.

Such education must not be only otherworldly, but must make its impact also upon all men and all nations with a contemporary evangel. It will not lose sight of the fact that the church's prime task is to challenge men and women individually in such numbers that the manifesto is global. As the world felt Hitler's threat at the borders of Czechoslovakia and Poland and England, and Mussolini's at the border of Greece, so too must it feel the promise of deliverance by Jesus at the fringe of our civilization, calling men to spiritual decision.

The Christian life must be lived out, among the regenerate, in every area of activity, until even the unregenerate are moved by Christian standards, acknowledging their force. The unregenerate are not, on that account, redeemed; nevertheless, they are more easily reached for Christ than those who have made a deliberate break with Christian standards, because they can be reminded that Christian ethics cannot be retained apart from Christian metaphysics. To the extent that any society is leavened with Christian conviction, it becomes a more hospitable environment for Christian expansion.

The evangelical mood must not withdraw from tomorrow's political scene. One can believe in separation of church and state, as do the Baptists, without sacrificing world statesmanship to men of godless convictions. The Roman Catholic church has trained its candidates for world diplomatic posts with singular vision; in today's world the ministry of world affairs is no less important than any other. Evangelicalism cannot remain silent, when society is being organized along the lines either of totalitarian absolutism or isolationist atomism; nor can it be content with a democratic way of life from which the redemptive element is abstracted. Always evangelicalism proclaims that the true center of a living community is God, known in His redemptive work through Jesus Christ; that kingships that ignore the true Lord of the universe are usurpative; that the value of human personality is guaranteed only in a redemptive context; that the liberties legitimately to be sought for man do not include a secularistic freedom from God; that without a transcendent spiritual ground in the living Redeemer no government can surmount the threat of disintegration.

Evangelicalism must not make the mistake, so common in our day, of regarding Communism or state Socialism as the adequate rectification of the errors of totalitarianism or the inadequacies of democracism. No political or economic system has utopian promise if the essential redemptive ingredient is missing from it. A redemptive totalitarianism is far preferable to an unredemptive democracy; a redemptive Communism far more advantageous than an unredemptive Capitalism, and vice versa. But the very element which is abstracted from currently proposed solutions is this redemptive element. The evangelical task will be to reproclaim it. No economic reorganization, however much it overcomes the antithesis of absolutism and individualism, is on that account to be identified with the kingdom of God and, further, only in a redemptive context can the antithesis be perfectly overcome. Communism may have more interest in individual rights than does Fascism, but it is no more to be identified with a Christian culture than is the democratic way of life. For it is the redemptive element that distinguishes Christianity, and it is the redemptive element that the jaded world culture so sorely needs.

Evangelicalism will be presumed not to have a mind on great world issues unless it speaks, but there is no justification for evangelical attempt at solution in non-redemptive frameworks. These have been tried and found wanting; let evangelicalism now speak the redemptive mind.

An efficient united nations organization may go a long way toward world peace, but it is not the best nor a permanent guarantee. Sharing the atom-bomb secret may go a long way toward removing international suspicions, but it is neither the best nor a lasting remover. Sacrificial distribution of food and clothing to the world's naked and starving multitudes may spare countless lives, but it does not provide a superlife which makes existence meaningful. Increasing the laborer's pay may remove some of the inequities of labor-management relations, but it makes no provision beyond the needs of the economic man.

What attitude then shall the evangelical take toward important modern attacks on deep-seated world problems when such efforts do not go deep enough to retain significance for the very improvements they seek to accomplish? This problem remains to be considered.

Of the necessity for a redemptive framework the evangelical has no doubt. But those who work for lesser reforms, and outside of that framework, will expect him to be on the side of right. What should be evangelicalism's attitude then?

CHAPTER VII

The Evangelical
"Formula of Protest"

The future kingdom in evangelical thought, it has already been insisted, does not displace an interim world program. That contemporary program in evangelicalism is (1) predicated upon an all-inclusive redemptive context for its assault upon global ills; (2) involves total opposition to all moral evils, whether societal or personal; (3) offers not only a higher ethical standard than any other system of thought, but provides also in Christ a dynamic to lift humanity to its highest level of moral achievement.

But the spearhead of the current attack on moral evils is not directed, as we have observed, by evangelical forces. Rather, the non-evangelical humanistic movements are heading up the agitation for a new and better world. The social program is, by and large, projected constructively today by non-evangelical groups.

Yet the non-evangelical camp has been plunged into considerable confusion, at the moment, by the collapse of its vision for an utopian world. The convictions of non-evangelicals are on the move; liberals are moving upward toward neo-supernaturalism or downward toward humanism, and some humanists are moving downward toward pessimism, while some others are impatiently marking time.

This creates the most favorable opportunity evangelicalism has had since its embarrassing divorce from a world social program, to recapture its rightful leadership in pressing for a new world order. Any conviction of foredoomed failure does not automatically cancel the missionary obligation. The futility of trying to win all does not mean that it is futile to try to win some areas of influence and life. An evangelical world program has its timeliest opportunity at the present hour.[1]

But a difficult problem is projected by the fact that evangelicals are found in fellowships which often seek elimination of social evils in a context which is not specifically redemptive, and often hostile to supernatural redemptionism. Since the evangelicals are convinced that a non-redemptive attack on any problem is sentenced to failure, what would be a consistent attitude

1. The difficulty of relating the Christian social imperative to concrete decisions is acknowledged by spokesmen for higher liberalism also. John C. Bennett suggests some of the problems in *Christian Ethics and Social Policy*, chapter two. But difficulty is no excuse for indifference.

in such circumstances? This is not an easy question to answer, and the writer does not pretend to offer more than preliminary reflection with regard to it. But it is a problem which confronted the apostolic church, and with the desupernaturalization of western culture it again looms large. The best evangelical thought may well occupy itself with the query in the immediate present. The spirit of the evangelical seminaries and colleges may largely determine the interpretation of social need which crystallizes during this post-war crisis period among Fundamentalist leaders. No framework is really relevant today unless it has an answer to the problem of sin and death in every area of human activity. Confronted by this problem, the evangelical mind will have to work out a satisfactory solution proportionate to its conviction of evangelical relevance.

The statement of a few pertinent considerations, however preliminary, may contribute to the ultimate solution, whether by action or reaction. Surely Christianity ought not to oppose any needed social reform. It ought, indeed, to be in the forefront of reformative attack. And it ought, if it has a historical consciousness, to press its attack on a redemption foundation, convinced that every other foundation for betterment, because of inherent weaknesses, cannot sustain itself.

While the evangelical will resist the non-evangelical formulas for solution, he assuredly ought not on that account to desist from battle against world evils. Just because his ideology is unalterably opposed to such evils, the evangelical should be counted upon not only to "go along" with all worthy reform movements, but to give them a proper leadership. He must give unlimited expression to his condemnation of all social evils, coupled with an insistence that a self-sustaining solution can be found only on a redemptive foundation. More vigorously than the humanists and religious modernists press their battle, the evangelical ought to be counted upon in the war against aggressive conflict, political naturalism, racial intolerance, the liquor traffic, labor-management inequities, and every wrong. And as vigorously as the evangelical presses his battle, he ought to be counted upon to point to the redemption that is in Christ Jesus as the only adequate solution. This appears to the writer to be the true evangelical methodology; to fill this form with content, in its application, is the difficult task which remains undone.

Evangelical action is not complicated within movements or organisms composed entirely of historic Christian theists, who, therefore, are united not only on the need for a social program, but also on the context within which such world renewal is a possibility. And yet only a minimal effort has been made in such circles, to articulate the Christian message in its social challenge. There are here and there conservative denominational groups, like the Reformed movements and the great

Southern Baptist Convention, which have maintained or are beginning to reflect a vigorous social interest. But to capture for the church all of the social zeal through redemptive categories, would involve even here a considerable change.

But the problem of social reform is more complicated when projected in great assemblies, often religious in nature, in which the membership is composed on inclusive lines, so that evangelicals, liberals, and humanists must act together. The evangelical voice in such a group cannot maintain silence when evils are condemned by others. But neither can it yield to a non-evangelical framework. Therefore, the path of evangelical action seems to be an eagerness to condemn all social evils, no less vigorously than any other group, and a determination (1) when evangelicals are in the majority, to couple such condemnation with the redemptive Christian message as the only true solution; (2) when evangelicals are in the minority, to express their opposition to evils in a "formula of protest," concurring heartily in the assault on social wrongs, but insisting upon the regenerative context as alone able to secure a permanent rectification of such wrongs. Thus evangelicals will take their stand against evil, and against it in the name of Jesus Christ the deliverer, both within their own groups and within other groups. To do this, is to recapture the evangelical spirit. Just how to express such protest in a positive rather than nega-

THE UNEASY CONSCIENCE OF MODERN FUNDAMENTALISM

tive way, beyond a minority committee report, remains to be studied. Every provision of democratic parliamentary procedure must be graciouly employed, rather than to misrepresent evangelical conviction at this point. Fundamentalists, uneasy about ecclesiastical bondage, are usually more alert to what they oppose, than to what they propose.

There are Fundamentalists who will insist immediately that no evangelical has a right to unite with non-evangelicals in any reform. It is not the task of this volume to evaluate the possibility or impossibility of evangelical loyalty to Christ within large modern denominations, each differing somewhat in organization and condition. Assuredly, no demand for loyalty can be recognized by the evangelical as higher than that by Christ Jesus, and each evangelical must settle, to the satisfaction of his own conscience, whether such loyalty is best served, or is impeded by loyalty within his denomination. But unrestricted loyalty to Christ cannot be interpreted as consistent with a tacit condonement of great world evils.

Apart from denominational problems, it remains true that the evangelical, in the very proportion that the culture in which he lives is not actually Christian, must unite with non-evangelicals for social betterment if it is to be achieved at all, simply because the evangelical forces do not predominate. To say that evangelicalism should not voice its convictions in a non-evangelical environment is simply to rob evangelicalism of its missionary vision.

It will be impossible for the evangelical to cooperate for social betterment with any group only when that group clearly rules out a redemptive reference as a live option for the achievement of good ends. If evangelicals in such groups are not accorded the democratic parliamentary right of minority action, there remains no recourse but that of independent action. Action there must be if evangelicalism is to recapture the spirit of its evangel. In non-evangelical groups, the evangelical must have opportunity to witness to the redemptive power of Jesus. Because of his convictions, he ought never to vote for something lower than his position except with an accompanying protest. This is a far truer road of expression for his convictions than to decline to support an attack on admitted evils — because the latter course tacitly withdraws his opposition to that which the Redeemer would unhesitatingly condemn.

In point of fact, those movements for a "pure evangelicalism," which have come out of larger denominational groups, have not infrequently done so with a sacrifice of social vision and a concentration on redemptive rescue of individuals from an environment conceded to be increasingly hostile. The point here is not that they needed to become socially indifferent as a consequence of a rupture with denominationalism, but rather

that such movements so frequently sacrifice an evangelical ecumenicity, and replace a world view with a fragmentary isolationism that "breaks through" its adverse environment with
atomistic missionary effort, at home and abroad, with whatever heroic and genuine sacrifices.

It cannot be held then that the social indifference of evangelicals is attributable to organic denominational associations
with liberalism. For Fundamentalist churches in no liberal association whatever are often as socially inactive as others. Cu-
riously, some Fundamentalist churches in liberal associations
have had more ecumenical awareness by far than many
churches in purely evangelical environments.

And yet it remains true that evangelical convictions need a
united voice; the force of the redemptive message will not break
with apostolic power upon the modern scene unless the American Council of Churches and the National Association of Evangelicals meet at some modern Antioch, and Peter and Paul are
face to face in a spirit of mutual love and compassion. If, as is often remarked, the Federal Council of Churches is the voice of
Protestant liberalism in America, Protestant evangelicalism too
needs a single voice. When such a unity comes, the present com-
petitive spirit of evangelical groups shall be overruled to the
glory of God, and the furtherance of the Gospel witness. If this
does not come, groups most responsible will inevitably wither.

CHAPTER VIII

The Dawn of a New Reformation

The need for a vital evangelicalism is proportionate to the world need. The days are as hectic as Nero's Rome, and they demand attention as immediate as Luke's Macedonia.

The cries of suffering humanity today are many. No evangelicalism which ignores the totality of man's condition dares respond in the name of Christianity. Though the modern crisis is not basically political, economic or social — fundamentally it is religious — yet evangelicalism must be armed to declare the implications of its proposed religious solution for the politico-economic and sociological context for modern life.

However marred, the world vessel of clay is not without some of the influence of the Master Molder. God has not left Himself entirely without witness in the global calamity; He discloses Himself in the tragedies as well as the triumphs of history. He works in history as well as above history. There is a universal confrontation of men and women by the divine Spirit, invading all cultures and all individual lives. There is a constructive work of God in history, even where the redemptive Gospel does not do a recreating work. The evangelical missionary message cannot be measured for success by the number of converts only. The Christian message has a salting effect upon the earth. It aims at a re-created society; where it is resisted, it often encourages the displacement of a low ideology by one relatively higher. Democratic humanitarianism furnishes a better context for human existence than political naturalism, except as it degenerates to the latter.

Modern evangelicalism need not substitute as its primary aim the building of "relatively higher civilizations." To do that is to fall into the error of yesterday's liberalism. Its supreme aim is the proclamation of redeeming grace to sinful humanity; there is no need for Fundamentalism to embrace liberalism's defunct social gospel. The divine order involves a supernatural principle, a creative force that enters society from outside its natural sources of uplift, and regenerates humanity. In that divine reversal of the self-defeating sinfulness of man is the only real answer to our problems — of whatever political, economic, or sociological nature. Is there political unrest? Seek first, not a Republican victory, or a labor victory, but the kingdom of God and His righteousness. Then there will be added — not necessarily a Republican or labor victory, but — political rest. Is there economic unrest? Seek first, not an increase of labor wages coupled with shorter hours, with its probable dog-eat-dog resultant of increased commodity cost, but the divine righteousness; this latter norm will involve fairness for both labor and management. But there will be added not only the solution of the problems of the economic man, but also those of the spiritual man. There is no satisfying rest for modern civilization if it is found in a context of spiritual unrest. This is but another way of declaring that the Gospel of redemption is the most pertinent message for our modern weariness, and that many of our other so-called solutions are quite impertinent, to say the least.

But that does not mean that we cannot cooperate in securing relatively higher goods, when this is the loftiest commitment we can evoke from humanity, providing we do so with appropriate warning of the inadequacy and instability of such solutions. The supernatural regenerative grace of God, proffered to the regenerate, does not prevent His natural grace to all men, regenerate and unregenerate alike. Because He brings rivers of living water to the redeemed, He does not on that account withhold the rain from the unjust and just alike. The realm of special grace does not preclude the realm of common grace. Just so, without minimizing the redemptive message, the church ministers by its message to those who stop short of commitment, as well as to regenerate believers.

The implications of this for evangelicalism seem clear. The battle against evil in all its forms must be pressed unsparingly; we must pursue the enemy, in politics, in economics, in science, in ethics — everywhere, in every field, we must pursue relentlessly. But when we have singled out the enemy — when we have disentangled him from those whose company he has kept and whom he has misled — we must meet the foe head-on, girt in the Gospel armor. Others may resist him with inadequate weapons; they do not understand aright the nature of the foe, nor the requirements for victory. We join with them in battle, seeking all the while more clearly to delineate the enemy, and more precisely to state the redemptive formula.

These sub-Christian environments which result from an intermingling of Christian and non-Christian elements, however much they fail to satisfy the absolute demand of God, are for the arena of life more satisfactory than an atmosphere almost entirely devoid of its redemptive aspects. It is far easier, in an idealistic context, to proclaim the essential Christian message, than it is in a thoroughly naturalistic context. Life means more in a context of idealism, because true meaning evaporates in a context of naturalism; for that reason, the preaching of a more abundant life finds a more favorable climate in the former. Though neither is to be identified with the kingdom of God, Anglo-Saxon democracy is a relatively better atmosphere by far than German totalitarianism was, and what made it better is the trace of Hebrew-Christian ideology that lingers in it.

While it is not the Christian's task to correct social, moral and political conditions as his primary effort apart from a redemptive setting, simply because of his opposition to evils he ought to lend his endorsement to remedial efforts in any context not specifically anti-redemptive, while at the same time decrying the lack of a redemptive solution. In our American environment, the influences of Christian theism are still abroad with enough vigor that the usual solutions are non-redemptive, rather than anti-redemptive, in character. Such cooperation, coupled with the Gospel emphasis, might provide the needed pattern of action for condemning aggressive warfare in concert with the United Nations Organization, while at the same time disputing the frame of reference by which the attempt is made to outlaw such warfare; for condemning racial hatred and intolerance, while at the same time protesting the superficial view of man which overlooks the need of individual regeneration; for condemning the liquor traffic, while insisting that it is impossible by legislation actually to correct the heart of man; for seeking justice for both labor and management in business and industrial problems, while protesting the fallacy that man's deepest need is economic. This is to link the positive Christian message with a redemptive challenge to the world on its bitterest fronts. Christian ethics will always resist any reduction of the good of the community to something divorced from theism and revelation; its conviction that non-evangelical humanism cannot achieve any lasting moral improvements in the world as a whole, because of the lack of an adequate dynamic, will engender the vigorous affirmation of a Christian solution.

Not that evangelical action stops here; this is hardly the beginning of it. One of the fallacies of modern thought, with which non-evangelical groups have been so much taken up in recent years, is that the mere "passing of a resolution" or the "writing of a book" in which the proposed method was set forth, automatically constitutes a long step on the road to deliverance. But too often the action stopped with the resolution or the book. Western culture was flooded with solutions for deliverance, from every sort of idealism and humanism, during the very years that it walked most rapidly to its doom. The same danger attends any evangelical revival.

The evangelical task primarily is the preaching of the Gospel, in the interest of individual regeneration by the supernatural grace of God, in such a way that divine redemption can be recognized as the best solution of our problems, individual and social. This produces within history, through the regenerative work of the Holy Spirit, a divine society that transcends national and international lines. The corporate testimony of believers, in their purity of life, should provide for the world an example of the divine dynamic to overcome evils in every realm. The social problems of our day are much more complex than in apostolic times, but they do not on that account differ in principle. When the twentieth century church begins to "out-live" its environment as the first century church out-reached its pagan neighbors, the modern mind, too, will stop casting about for other solutions. The great contemporary problems are moral and spiritual. They demand more than a formula. The evangelicals have a conviction of absoluteness concerning their message, and not to proclaim it, in the assault on social evils, is sheer inconsistency. But the modern mood is far more likely to react first on the level of Christianity as a life view, than at the level of Christianity as a world view. Obviously, from the evangelical viewpoint, the two cannot be divorced. But from the non-evangelical viewpoint, a baptism of pentecostal fire resulting in a world missionary program and a divinely-empowered Christian community would turn the uneasy conscience of modern evangelicalism into a new reformation — this time with ecumenical significance.